MW00917224

The Breath of God

A Study of the Holy Spirit

By

Richard A. Ingui

Brook Cherith Media
12 Corporate Drive
Clifton Park, New York 12065

Copyright © 2006 by Richard A. Ingui

Breath of God
by Richard A. Ingui

Printed in the United States of America

ISBN 1-59781-996-4

All rights reserved solely by the author. The author guar-
antees all contents are original and do not infringe upon
the legal rights of any other person or work. No part of this
publication may be reproduced, stored in a retrieval system,
or transmitted in any form or by any other means, electronic,
mechanical, photocopying, recording r otherwise without
prior permission of the author. The views expressed in this
book are not necessarily those of the publisher.

Unless otherwise indicated, all Scripture quotations are taken
from the New King James version of the Bible. © Copyright
1982 Thomas Nelson, Inc.

NIV – New International Version © 1985, 1995, 2002 The
Zondervan Corporation

www.xulonpress.com

Dedication

This book is dedicated to my loving wife and partner, Nancy. She has been supportive in this endeavor from the beginning. And her enthusiasm for this work has kept me focused on finalizing my effort.

Nancy is also my co-laborer at River of Hope Fellowship. She has been a blessing, not only to me, but also to our body.

Sunshine, this work is dedicated to you.

Contents

Chapter 1

Is the Holy Spirit God?

There has been much confusion over the Holy Spirit, also known as the Holy Ghost. Who, or what, exactly is the Holy Spirit. Is the Holy Spirit, God or some force emanating from God? Is the Holy Spirit an entity, or a person? We will answer these questions, and others, as we study the Holy Spirit.

Is the Holy Spirit God?

Well, in order for the Holy Spirit to be God, He must meet the definition of God. God is defined as all powerful (omnipotent), all knowing (omniscient), all present (omni-present), and eternal.

The first criteria is that God is all powerful. We see in Luke 1:35, the angel Gabriel responds to Mary concerning the conception of Jesus saying, "The Holy Spirit will come upon you, and the power of the Highest will overshadow you; therefore, also, that the Holy One who is to be born will be called the Son of God." Here we see that the power and the might of God Himself is bestowed on the Holy Spirit. Only God can create life and in Job 33:4, we see the Holy Spirit active in creation: "The Spirit of God has made me, and the breath of the Almighty gives me life." Scripture tell us that the Holy Spirit is omnipotent.

The next criterion is that God is all knowing. In 1 Corinthians 2:10-11, it says, "But God has revealed them to us through His Spirit. For the Spirit searches all things, yes, the deep things of God. For what man knows the things of a man except the spirit of the man which is in him? Even so no one knows the things of God except the Spirit of God." The Spirit searches and examines all things. Yes, even the depths of God. Therefore, whatever God knows, the Holy Spirit knows! And God knows everything.

The next criterion is that God is all present. The Old Testament tells us the Spirit is everywhere. In Psalm 139:7-10, it states, "Where can I go from Your Spirit? Or where can I flee from Your presence? If I ascend into heaven, You are there; if I make my bed in Hell, behold, You are there; If I take the wings of the morning, and dwell in the uttermost parts of the sea, even there your hand shall lead me, and Your right hand shall hold me." Clearly the Holy Spirit is omnipresent.

The final criterion is that God is eternal. Hebrews 9:14 says, "...how much more shall the blood of Christ, who through the eternal Spirit offered Himself without spot to God...." Here we see that the Holy Spirit is eternal.

Scripture tells us clearly that the Holy Spirit meets all the requirements of God. Therefore the Holy Spirit truly is God and part of the Trinity.

The Holy Spirit is called God in Scripture.

Besides meeting the definition of God, the name of the Holy Spirit is coupled with God in the Scriptures. In Matthew 28:19, we see the Holy Spirit being associated with the Father and the Son. It says, "Go therefore and make disciples of all nations, baptizing them in the *name of the Father and of the Son and of the Holy Spirit.*" Also in 2 Corinthians 13:14,

Paul writes, "*The grace of the Lord Jesus Christ, and the love of God, and the communion of the Holy Spirit* be with you all, amen." Also, the Holy Spirit is actually called God in Scripture. Ananias apparently took an oath to the Holy Spirit concerning the sale of his land. As Acts 5:3-4 states, "But Peter said, 'Ananias, why has Satan filled your heart *to lie to the Holy Spirit* and keep back part of the price of the land for yourself? While it remained, was it not your own? And after it was sold, was it not in your own control? Why have you conceived this thing in your heart? *You have not lied to men, but to God.*'"

So we see several examples of the Holy Spirit being called God.

The Holy Spirit is separate from Jesus and the Lord.

We see that the Holy Spirit is God, yet He is separate and distinct from the Father and the Son. In Luke 3:21-22, we see that the Holy Spirit was actually physically separate as He descended from heaven: "Now when all the people were baptized, it came to pass that Jesus also was baptized; and while He prayed, the heaven was opened. And *the Holy Spirit descended in bodily form like a dove upon Him, and a voice from heaven which said:* 'You are My beloved Son; in you I am well pleased.'" This passage clearly states that Jesus was on Earth, the Father was in heaven, and the Holy Ghost descended from heaven.

Although the Holy Spirit is God, there is an authority structure in Heaven. It is God the Father at the head, then Jesus, then the Holy Spirit. In John 14:16, Scripture reveals that the Holy Spirit was sent by God at the request of Jesus: "*And I will ask the Father, and he will give you another Counselor* to be with you forever-" Also in John 15:26, it says, "When the *Counselor comes, whom I will send to you from the Father*, the Spirit of truth, who goes out from the Father, he will testify about me." And in John 16:13,14, it states, "However, when He, the Spirit of truth, has come, He will guide you into all truth; for *He will not speak on His own authority, but whatever He hears He will speak; and He will tell you things to come. He will glorify Me, for He will take of what is Mine and declare it to you.*"

So we see that the Holy Spirit is fully God, yet under the authority of the Father and Jesus. You can't send someone who isn't under authority to you.

Chapter 2

Is the Holy Spirit a Person?

We know the Holy Spirit is God, but what exactly is He like? Is He a person, or some spiritual force? Let's look at His characteristics, which will define Him.

Some of the distinctive characteristics of a personality are Knowledge, Will, and Emotions or Feelings. The Holy Spirit has a distinct personality, which is described in Scripture.

Clearly, the Holy Spirit has KNOWLEDGE. In 1 Corinthians 2:10-11, Paul shows us that the Holy Spirit knows everything God knows: "But God has revealed them to us through His Spirit. For the Spirit searches all things, yes, the deep things of God. For what man knows the things of a man except the spirit of the man, which is in him? *Even so no one knows the things of God except the Spirit of God.*"

The Spirit has a WILL. In 1 Corinthians 12:11, we see that the Spirit determines or wills who receives spiritual gifts: "But one and the same *Spirit works all these things, distributing to each one individually as He wills.*"

Also, the Spirit of God has a MIND. Romans 8:27 clearly states that the Holy Spirit has His own mind: "Now He who searches the hearts *knows what the mind of the Spirit* is, because He makes intercession for the saints according to the will of God."

The Holy Spirit expresses EMOTIONS. LOVE is shown in Romans 15:30, "Now I beg you, brethren, through the Lord Jesus Christ, and *through the love of the Spirit,* that you strive together with me in your prayers to God for me." GRIEVING is demonstrated in Ephesians 4:30, "And *do not grieve the Holy Spirit of God,* by whom you were sealed for the day of redemption."

There is an interaction with the Holy Spirit. He not only expresses emotions, He also feels them. Scripture tells us that the Holy Spirit can be rebelled against, grieved, lied to, and blasphemed. He is rebelled against and grieved in Isaiah 63:10, "*But they rebelled and grieved His Holy Spirit;* so He turned Himself against them as an enemy, and He fought against them." He is lied to in Acts 5:3: "But Peter said, 'Ananias, why has Satan filled your heart *to lie to the Holy Spirit* and keep back part of the price of the land for yourself?'" Jesus is very clear in Mathew 12:31-32 not to blaspheme the Holy Spirit: "Therefore I say to you, every sin and blasphemy will be forgiven men, *but the blasphemy against the Spirit will not be forgiven men.* Anyone who speaks a word against the Son of Man, it will be forgiven him; but whoever speaks against the Holy Spirit, it will not be forgiven him, either in this age or the age to come." We must be careful to treat the Spirit of God with love and respect not only on Sunday, but in our daily lives as well.

The Holy Spirit responds to us in many different ways.

The Holy Spirit searches God's wisdom; speaks of this wisdom to the churches; cries out in our hearts; intercedes for us; testifies of Christ; and teaches and guides us. All attributes of a person.

The Holy Spirit searches the deep things of God.

In 1 Corinthians 2:10, it says, "But God has revealed them to us through His Spirit. *For the Spirit searches all things, yes, the deep things of God.*"

He speaks to us of His wisdom.

In Revelations 2:7, it says, "He who has an ear, let him hear *what the Spirit says to the churches.* To him who overcomes, I will give to eat from the tree of life, which is in the midst of the Paradise of God."

He cries out in our hearts.

Paul writes in Galatians 4:6, "And because you are sons, God has sent forth the *Spirit of His Son into your hearts, crying out, 'Abba, Father!'*"

The Holy Spirit prays for us.

It states in Romans 8:26, "Likewise the Spirit also helps in our weaknesses. For we do not know what we should pray for as we ought, but the *Spirit Himself makes intercession for us with groanings which cannot be uttered.*"

He testifies of Jesus.

It says in John 15:26, "But when the Helper comes, whom I shall send to you from the Father, the Spirit of truth who proceeds from the Father, *He will testify of Me.*"

He is a teacher. As it states in John 14:26, "But the Helper, the Holy Spirit, whom the Father will send in My name, *He will teach you all things,* and bring to your remembrance all things that I said to you."

The Holy Spirit is our Guide. In John 16:12-15, it says, "I still have many things to say to you, but you cannot bear them now. However, when He, *the Spirit of truth, has come, He will guide you into all truth*; for He will not speak on His own authority, but whatever He hears He will speak; and He will tell you things to come. He will glorify Me, for He will take of what is Mine and declare it to you. All things that the Father has are Mine. Therefore I said that He will take of Mine and declare it to you." If we are willing to listen and follow God, the Holy Spirit will provide direction for our lives. In Romans 8:14, Paul states, *"For as many as are led by the Spirit of God, these are sons of God."* Also in Acts 16:6-7, Paul and his companions were given very specific guidance by the Spirit of God.

Chapter 3

The Names and Symbols of the Holy Spirit

The Holy Spirit is referred to by at least 25 different names in both the Old and New Testaments.

Both the Greek and Hebrew words for *The Spirit* translate literally as "Breath" or "Wind."

Both translations are applied to the Holy Spirit. The concept of breath is found in John 20:22. After His resurrection, Jesus addresses the apostles: "And when He had said this, He *breathed* on them, and said to them, *"Receive the Holy Spirit."* In Job 33:4, it says, *"The Spirit of God has made me; the breath of the Almighty gives me life."* The Spirit is God's breath pouring life into us.

The Holy Spirit is characterized as the *"Wind".*

This reference is found in John 3:6-8, and it says, "That which is born of flesh is flesh, and that which is born of the Spirit is spirit. Do not marvel that I said to you 'You must be born again.' *The wind* blows where it wishes, and you hear the sound of it, but cannot tell where it comes from and where it goes. So is everyone who is born of the Spirit." Here the Greek word "pneuma" is used interchangeably with wind and spirit. This gives a clear image of the Holy Spirit.

"Oil" is used to describe the Holy Spirit.

In Isaiah 61:1, it states, *"The Spirit of Lord God is upon Me, because the Lord has anointed Me* to preach good tidings to the poor." Oil was commonly used to anoint kings and priests as a symbol of empowerment by the Holy Spirit.

The Spirit of God is depicted as a "Dove".

In Matthew 3:16, it says, "Then Jesus, when He had been baptized, came up immediately from the water; and behold, the heavens were opened to Him, and *He saw the Spirit of God descending like a dove and alighting upon Him.*"

Water is also used as a description.

In John 7:38-39, Jesus states, "He who believes in Me, as the Scripture has said, *out of his heart will flow rivers of living water.' But this He spoke concerning the Spirit, whom those believing in Him would receive*; for the Holy Spirit was not yet given, because Jesus was not yet glorified." Scripture also depicts the Holy Spirit as "rain" , "dew", and "springs."

The symbol of Fire is used.

In Acts 2:3-4, it says, "The there appeared to them divided tongues, *as of fire*, and one sat upon each of them. And they were all *filled with the Holy Spirit* and began to speak with other tongues, as the Spirit gave them utterance."

The Spirit of God.

In 1 Corinthians 3:16 we see the *direct association with God*. "Do you not know that you are the temple of God and that the *Spirit of God dwells in you?"*

The Spirit of the Lord.

The same association is found in the Old Testament. In Isaiah 11:2, it says, "*The Spirit of the Lord* shall rest upon Him, The Spirit of wisdom and of understanding, the Spirit of counsel and might, the Spirit of knowledge and of the fear of the Lord."

The Spirit of the Living God.

In 2 Corinthians 3:3 we see Paul write about a *living God*, not one who exists only in scripture, but one who lives in our hearts. "You are manifestly an epistle of Christ, ministered by us, written not with ink but by *the Spirit of the living God,* not on tablets of stone but on tablets of flesh, that is, of the heart."

The Spirit of Christ.

Romans 8:9 tells us "But you are not in the flesh but in the Spirit, if indeed the Spirit of God dwells in you. Now if anyone does not have *the Spirit of Christ,* he is not His." Also the Spirit of Jesus Christ in Philippians 1:19; the Spirit of Jesus in Acts 16:6,7; the Spirit of His Son in Galatians 4:6.

The Holy Spirit.

The name which we are most familiar is found in Luke 11:13 "If you then, being evil, know how to give good gifts to your children, how much more will your heavenly Father give the Holy Spirit to those who ask Him!" This name emphasizes the essential moral character of the Spirit. *He is Holy in Himself.*

The Spirit of Holiness.

In Romans 1:4, it states, "And declared to be the Son of God with power, according to the *Spirit of holiness,* by the resurrection from the dead." The name, Spirit of Holiness, implies that the Holy Spirit is not merely holy Himself, but *imparts holiness to others.*

The Spirit of Truth.

The Holy Spirit is referred to as the Spirit of Truth in John 14:17 *"Even the Spirit of truth,* whom the world cannot receive, because it neither sees Him nor knows Him; but you know Him, for he dwells with you and will be in you." *It is the work of the Holy spirit to communicate truth and to impart this truth to us.*

The Counselor.

The Holy Spirit is referred to as the Counselor again and again in Scripture. In John 14:26, it states, "But the *Counselor,* the Holy Spirit, whom the Father will send in My name, will teach you all things, and will remind you of everything I have said to you."(NIV). The Greek word, para-kleetos, translates "one called alongside." The Holy Spirit is one called to stand constantly by our side and one who is ever ready to stand by us and take our part in everything in which His help is needed. Jesus is in heaven, and He has sent us a Counselor, who is just as divine, just as wise, just as loving, and just as ready to help us in our time of need.

Other interesting names that are found in Scripture are as follows:

Spirit of Jesus Christ (Phil. 1:19)
Spirit of His Son (Gal. 4:6)
Spirit of Promise (Eph. 1:13)
Spirit of Judgment (Isa. 4:4)
Spirit of Burning (Isa. 4:4)
Spirit of Wisdom and Understanding (Isa. 11:2)
Spirit of Counsel and Might (Isa. 11:2)
Spirit of Knowledge and the Fear of the Lord
(Isa. 11:2)

Spirit of Life (Rom. 8:2)
Spirit of Grace (Heb. 10:29)
Spirit of Grace and Supplication (Zeh. 12:10)
Spirit of Glory (1 Pet. 4:14)
Eternal Spirit (Heb. 9:14)
Oil of Gladness (Heb. 1:9)

The Holy Spirit is involved in the creation of the universe and of man. Job 33:4 states, "The Spirit of God has made me; *the breath of the Almighty gives me life.*" We have already seen that the breath of God is the Holy Spirit. Genesis 1:1-3 describes the Holy Spirit's presence in the creation of the universe. It is evident that the Father, Son, and Holy Spirit are all active in the creative work.

Chapter 4

What does the Holy Spirit do?

The Holy Spirit is involved in conviction of sin, aiding us to live righteously, and He convicts the world of judgment. He is also involved in renewal.

Conviction.

It is the work of the Holy Spirit to convict men of their sins, to convict us of Christ's righteousness, and to convict the world of God's judgment. In John 16:8-11, Jesus states: *"And when He has come, He will convict the world of sin, and of righteousness, and of judgment:* of sin, because they do not believe in Me; of righteousness because I go to My Father and you see Me no more; of judgment, because the ruler of this world is judged."

The sin that the Holy Spirit convicts man of is the sin of unbelief in Jesus Christ. Not the sin of stealing, lying, murder, adultery or any other deed, but the sin of unbelief in Jesus. The one sin that reveals man's rebellion against God and defiance of Him is not believing in the one He has sent. It is realization of this sin that convicted the 3000 on Pentecost.

The Holy Spirit convicts men of their sin and changes their hearts toward Christ. In Acts 2:36-37, Peter said "Therefore let all Israel be assured of this: God has made this Jesus, whom you crucified, both Lord and Christ.' *When the people heard this, they were cut to the heart* and said to Peter and the other apostles, 'Brothers, what shall we do?'" (NIV). Peter spoke these words after Pentecost, and was empowered by the Holy Spirit. It was the Holy Spirit that "cut to the heart," not Peter.

Although it is the Holy Spirit that convicts men of sin, He does it primarily through us. In chapter 10 of Acts, the Bible tells of the conversion of Cornelius and his family by the Holy Spirit through Peter. In Acts 10:44-46, it says, *"While Peter was speaking these words, the Holy Spirit came upon all who heard the message.* The circumcised believers who had come with Peter were astonished that the gift of the Holy Spirit had been poured out even on the Gentiles. For they heard them speaking in tongues and praising God." Peter recounts the experience to the apostles in Acts 11:15, *"And as I began to speak, the Holy Spirit fell upon them, as upon us at the beginning."* Although Paul's conversion was done directly by Jesus, his entire ministry was devoted to the testimony of Jesus Christ. The Holy Spirit's primary way to save the unbeliever is through those already saved!

The Holy Spirit convicts not only of sin, but also of righteousness.

In John 16:10, it says, *"in regard to righteousness, because I am going to the Father, where you can see me no longer"* (NIV). Righteousness is translated literally as "rightwiseness," the ability to live according to God's law, free from sin. With Jesus in heaven, the Holy Spirit was sent to aid us in living lives of righteousness. In John 16:13 Jesus states, *"However, when He, the Spirit of truth, has come, He will guide you into all truth;"* What is truth? Jesus is the truth! John 14:6 states, "Jesus said to him, '*I am the way, the truth and the life.* No one comes to the Father except through Me.'"

The Holy Spirit also convicts the world of judgment.

John 16:11 states, *"and in regard to judgment, because the prince of this world now stands condemned"* (NIV). The Lord has made it clear that Jesus' death on the cross was not the judgment of Christ, but the judgment of Satan. Also in John 12:30-32, it says, "Jesus answered and said, 'This voice did not come because of Me, but for your sake. *Now is the judgment of this world; now the ruler of this world will be cast out.* And I, if I am lifted up from the earth, will draw all people to myself.'" The Holy Spirit opens our eyes to accept this fact and convicts us that Satan stands defeated.

The Holy Spirit bears witness to Jesus Christ.

It is clear from Scripture that the work of the Holy Spirit is to bear witness to Jesus. In John 15:26-27, it states, *"But when the Helper comes, whom I shall send to you from the Father, the Spirit of truth who proceeds from the Father, He will testify of Me.* And you also will bear witness, because you have been with Me from the beginning." It is only through the Holy Spirit's *testimony* to our hearts that we ever come to really know Jesus Christ. No amount of reading the Word or listening to man's testimony will ever allow us to have a personal relationship with Christ. Only when the Holy Spirit himself takes the Word or testimony and speaks directly to our hearts, not our minds, will we really know Jesus. In 1 John 2:27, John talks about the anointing, or the Spirit. "But the anointing which you have received from Him abides in you, and you do not need anyone to teach you; but as the same anointing teaches you concerning all things, and is true, and is not a lie, and just as it has taught you, you will abide in Him." Also in 1 Corinthians 12:3, it says, "Therefore I make known to you that no one who is speaking by the Spirit of God calls Jesus accursed, and no one can say that Jesus is Lord except by the Holy Spirit." Scripture was inspired by the Holy Spirit, and only the Holy Spirit can make the Word pierce our hearts!

The renewal by the Holy Spirit.

The Holy Spirit renews men's lives. He imparts new spiritual lives to those dead to Christ. In Titus 3:5-6 it states, "He saved us, not because of righteous things we have done, but because of his mercy. He saved us through the washing of rebirth *and renewal by the Holy Spirit*, whom he poured out on us generously through Jesus Christ our Savior." Renewal starts by being born again. John says in 3:3-6, "Jesus answered and said to him, '*Most assuredly, I say to you, unless one is born again*, he cannot see the kingdom of God.' Nicodemus said to Him, 'How can a man be born when he is old? Can he enter a second time into his mother's womb to be born?' Jesus answered. 'Most assuredly, I say to you, *unless one is born of water and the Spirit, he cannot enter the kingdom of God*. That which is born of the flesh is flesh, and that which is born of the Spirit is spirit.'" Also in Romans 8:9, it says, "*But you are not in the flesh but in the Spirit*, if indeed the Spirit of God dwells in you. Now if anyone does not have the Spirit of Christ, he is not His." Unless we are renewed again by the Spirit, *we cannot know the things of God*. In 1 Corinthians 2:14, it states, "But the natural man does not receive the things of the Spirit of God, for they are foolishness to him; *nor can he know them, because they are spiritually discerned*."

Once you are born again, the Holy Spirit begins the renewal process.

Paul states in 1 Corinthians 6:11, "*But you were washed, but you were sanctified, but you were justified in the name of the Lord Jesus and by the Spirit of our God.*"

We must be strengthened by the Holy Spirit to live Godly lives. In Ephesians 3:16-19, it states, "That He would grant you, according to the riches of His glory, *to be strengthened with might through His Spirit in the inner man,* that Christ may dwell in your hearts through faith; that you, being rooted and grounded in love, may be able to comprehend with all the saints what is the width and length and depth and height - to know the love of Christ which passes knowledge; *that you may be filled with the fullness of God.*"

Renewal requires walking in the Spirit and resisting the flesh. Paul writes in Galatians 5:16-18, "I say then: '*Walk in the spirit, and you shall not fulfill the lust of the flesh. For the flesh lusts against the Spirit, and the Spirit against the flesh*; and these are contrary to one another, so that you do not do the things that you wish. But if you are led by the Spirit, you are not under the law.'"

How do we know we are walking in the Spirit? By the fruit of our lives. And what is the fruit that people can see? Paul states in Galatians 5:22-25, "*But the fruit of the Spirit is love, joy, peace, longsuffering, kindness, goodness, faithfulness, gentleness, self control.* Against such there is no law. And those who are Christ's have crucified the flesh with its passions and desires. *If we live in the Spirit, let us also walk in the Spirit.*"

Renewal begins with sanctification.

The renewal process begins with sanctification. Sanctification is the process by which we, as Christians, cleanse ourselves so that we may be more Christ-like. In 1 Thessalonians 2:13, Paul writes, "But we are bound to give thanks to God always for you, brethren beloved by the Lord, because God from the beginning chose you for salvation *through sanctification by the Spirit* and belief in the truth." Also in 1 Corinthians 6:1, it says, "And such were some of you. *But you were washed, but you were sanctified, but you were justified in the name of the Lord Jesus and by the Spirit of our God."*

Changes begin when we change our nature.

Our natural state is of the world. Galatians 5:19-21 states, "The acts of the sinful nature are obvious: sexual immorality, impurity and debauchery, idolatry and witchcraft, hatred, discord, jealousy, fits of rage, selfish ambition, dissension, factions and envy, drunkenness, orgies, and the like. I warn you, as I did before, that those who live like this will not inherit the kingdom of God." Paul goes on in verses 22 and 23 to describe the fruit of the Spirit. "But the fruit of the Spirit is love, joy, peace, patience, kindness, goodness, faithfulness, gentleness, and self control. Against such things there is no law." These divine qualities that Paul describes are attributes that are available to us through the help of the Holy Spirit. In 2 Peter 1:3-4, it states, "As *His divine power has given to us all things that pertain to life and godliness,* through the knowledge of Him who called us by glory and virtue, by which have been given to us exceedingly great and precious promises, *that through these you may be partakers of the divine nature,* having escaped the corruption that is in the world through lust." Partaking in this divine nature is a conscious decision, and must be practiced.

How does this all happen? By using our spiritual weapons!

Paul writes in 2 Corinthians 10:4-5, *"For the weapons of our warfare are not carnal but mighty in God* for pulling down strongholds, casting down arguments and every high thing that exalts itself against the knowledge of God, bringing every thought into captivity to the obedience of Christ." And what are these weapons? In Ephesians 6:17-18, it states, "And take the helmet of salvation, and *the sword of the Spirit, which is the Word of God; praying always with all prayer and supplication in the Spirit,* being watchful to this end with all perseverance and supplication for all the saints." Changes occur when we read the Word. Paul says in 2 Timothy 3:16-17, *"All Scripture is given by inspiration of God, and is profitable for doctrine, for reproof, for correction, for instruction in righteousness, that the man of God may be complete, thoroughly equipped for every good work."* Pray when we are weak. In Matthew 26:41 Jesus advises His disciples on praying. *"Watch and pray, lest you enter into temptation. The spirit is willing, but the flesh is weak."* Paul speaks of changes in the saints in Corinth. He points out that their conduct exemplifies the gospel. In 1 Corinthians 3:3, it states, "You show that you are a letter from Christ, the result of our ministry, *written not with ink but with the Spirit of the living God, not on tablets of stone but on tablets of human hearts"* (NIV). Outward changes occur when our inner nature is changed.

Chapter 5

The Holy Spirit Lives in Us!

Scripture tells us that *the Holy Spirit actually dwells within us*! In 1 Corinthians 6:19 Paul writes, "Or do you not know that *your body is the temple of the Holy Spirit* who is in you, whom you have from God, and you are not your own?" John states in 14:16-17, "And I will pray the Father, and He will give you another Helper, that He may abide with you forever, even the Spirit of truth, whom the world cannot receive, because it neither sees Him nor knows Him; but you know Him, *for He dwells with you and will be in you.*" It is clear that when we receive Christ, the Holy Spirit lives in us. However, this does not mean that we allow Him to take control of our lives! *We must allow Him to take possession of the whole person: spirit, soul and body.* The Holy Spirit dwells in us. We need to be considerate of the dwelling of a Holy and righteous God. *We must be careful in all things not to grieve Him, who dwells in us.*

The Holy Spirit is our source of a full and satisfying life.

Jesus said in John 4:14, "but whoever drinks of the water that I shall give him will never thirst. *But the water I shall give him will become in him a fountain of water springing*

31

up into everlasting life." Earthly water satisfies for awhile, but spiritual water lasts forever. John 7:37-39 says, "On the last day, that great day of the feast, Jesus stood and cried out saying, 'If anyone thirsts, let him come to Me and drink. *He who believes in Me, as the Scripture has said, out of his heart will flow rivers of living water.' By this He spoke concerning the Spirit, whom those believing in Him would receive*; for the Holy Spirit was not given, because Jesus was not yet glorified."

The Holy Spirit Forms Christ within Us.

In Ephesians 3:14-19 we see that the work of the Spirit is to *form the living Christ in us*; to see that *we are rooted and grounded in love;* to see that *we know the love of Christ;* to see that *we are filled with the fullness of God.* Ephesians 3:14-19 says, "For this reason I bow my knees to the Father of our Lord Jesus Christ, from whom the whole family in heaven and earth is named, that He would grant you, according to the riches of His glory, to be strengthen with might through His Spirit in the inner man, that *Christ may dwell in your hearts* through faith; that you, *being rooted and grounded in love*, may be able to comprehend with all the saints what is the *width and length and depth and height- to know the love of Christ* which passes knowledge; that *you may be filled with all the fullness of God.*"

The Holy Spirit strengthens our "inner" man with might (or power) so that Jesus would dwell in our hearts. In Ephesians 3:16-17, it states, "That He would grant you, according to the riches of His glory, to *be strengthen with might through His Spirit in the inner man, that Christ may dwell in your hearts through faith.*" The Greek word "katoikeo" means to dwell or abide, not just to live in a place for awhile, but to live in a place forever. For us to try to live a Christlike life by our own strength will only lead to disappointment and disillusionment. But God knows we cannot achieve this by our own power, and He does not ask the impossible. He offers to form Jesus in us by the power of the Holy Spirit. But the key is that we give control of our lives to the Spirit. We must *allow* Him to form Christ in us. He will not force Christ's nature on us. We must have open hearts!

The Holy Spirit's work is to "root and ground" our lives in love.

Expanding on Ephesians 3:16-19 " That He would grant you, according to the riches of His glory, to be strengthened with might (or power) through His Spirit in the inner man, that Christ may dwell (to settle down in a dwelling) in your hearts through faith; that you, being rooted and grounded (to lay the foundation) in love, may be able to comprehend (to understand or perceive) with all the saints what is the width (or breadth) and length, and depth (or deepness) and height (or summit) - to know the love of Christ which passes knowledge; that you may be filled (to be filled to the full) with all the fullness of God." Love is the key in our relationship to God and to one another. It is the work of the Holy Spirit to root and ground our lives in love. A plant's root system gives it life; it is the method that feeds and nourishes the plant. We need to send our "roots" into God's love. For it is there that we will find nourishment. God's love is the foundation to which we are attached - that will "ground" us in times of fierce winds. Having the full knowledge of God's love will hold us steady and keep us from being uprooted by storms. The Holy Spirit provides the power for us to root and ground our lives in love, which is God's true nature. To fully grasp the width and length and height and depth of Christ's love, we need the power of the Holy Spirit. In Ephesians 3:18-19, it states, "May be able to comprehend with all the saints what is the width and length, and depth and height- to know the love of Christ which passes knowledge." We cannot in our frail humanity ever expect to fully grasp all of God's love in our hearts. Intellectually, we may think we understand, but no one can truly explain all the many facets of love. It must be experienced. Christ's wondrous love must be written on our hearts by the Holy Spirit. It is the only way.

We have the ability to be filled to the measure with the fullness of God. In Ephesians 3:19, it says, "To know the love of Christ which passes knowledge; that you may be filled with all the fullness of God." This is an incredible statement - that the fullness of God is available to us, and that we may be filled to the measure!

Chapter 6

"Therefore by their fruits you will know them"

Jesus said in Matthew 7:20 that we will be known by our fruit. He was talking about how people perceive us treating other people. This why we are to exemplify the fruit of the Spirit.

The Holy Spirit brings forth Christ's character.

In Galatians 5:22-23 Paul tells us "But the fruit of the Spirit is love, joy, peace, longsuffering, kindness, goodness, faithfulness, gentleness, self-control. Against such there is no law." Here we see the "fruit of the Spirit." All the wonderful characteristics of Christ are available to us from the Holy Spirit, if we give Him control of our lives. Just as natural fruit is good for our inner man, also fruits of the Spirit are good for the "inner" man. The products of the Spirit bring nourishment to the soul. Also, they are the fruit, not fruits, of the Spirit. The Holy Spirit does not give joy to one and peace to another. All are available to each of us!

The fruit of the Spirit is love: agape love, which is God's love, not man's love. It is joy: a deep seeded joy. It is peace: resting in Christ. It is longsuffering: to endure knowing God's in control. It is kindness: to be kind, gentle, and merciful. It is goodness: to be of benefit to your neighbor. It is faithfulness: to be faithful and steadfast. It is gentleness: to be gracious and kind. And it is self-control: to not let worldly nature take over. In your fellowship with the Holy Spirit ask Him to give you these wonderful fruits, and you will find your character becoming more like Christ's.

The fruit of the Spirit is evidence of Christ within us. The word fruit is used to describe the characteristics of Jesus, which are manifested in us by the Holy Spirit. Paul uses "fruit," not "fruits," meaning all are available to each of us. Not love to one, or joy to another. In Matthew 7:16-20, Jesus states, "You will know them by their fruits. Do men gather grapes from thornbushes or figs from thistles? Even so, every good tree bears good fruit, but a bad tree bears bad fruit. A good tree cannot bear bad fruit, nor can a bad tree bear good fruit. Every tree that does not bear good fruit is cut down and thrown into the fire. Therefore *by their fruits you will know them.*"

Characteristics of the fruit of the Spirit—love

Love (the Greek is "agape") is one characteristic that all the other fruits draw on. It is the very essence of God. In 1 John 4:7-8, it states, "Beloved, let us love one another, for love is of God; and everyone who loves is born of God and knows God. 8 He who does not love does not know God, for God is love." God's love enters our hearts through the Holy Spirit and changes us forever. In Romans 5:5, Paul writes, "Now hope does not disappoint, because *the love of God has been poured out in our hearts by the Holy Spirit who was given to us.*" It is the kind of love that is given even though it is not deserved. In Romans 5:8, it says, "But God demonstrates His own love for toward us, in that while we were still sinners, Christ died for us." We are inseparable from the love of God (Romans 8:35-39). Loving one another is not optional. Jesus said in John 13:34-35, "A new commandment I give to you, that you love one another; as I have loved you, that you also love one another. By this all will know that you are My disciples if you have love for one another." Paul clearly defines love in 1 Corinthians 13:4-7, "Love suffers long and is kind; love does not envy; love does not parade itself, is not puffed up; does not behave rudely, does not seek its own, is not provoked, thinks no evil; does not rejoice in iniquity, but rejoices in the truth; bears all things, believes all things, hopes all things, endures all things."

The love that the Holy Spirit produces is beyond human love. It is *the love of God that flows through us.* Love is the foundation that all the other fruits of the Spirit are built on. To be truly filled with the Spirit is to be filled with love and to show this love to the world.

Characteristics of the fruit of the Spirit—joy

Joy is that deep, meaningful rejoicing because of God's presence in us. In Philippians 4:4, Paul writes, "Rejoice *in the Lord always. Again I will say, rejoice!*" In Psalm 16:11, it says, "*In thy presence is fullness of joy.*" This joy is as a result of our relationship with God. It is not the result of any earthly relationship. In Romans 14:17, it says, "For the kingdom of God is not food and drink, but righteousness and peace and *joy in the Holy Spirit.*" Jesus said in John 15:11, "These things I have spoken to you, that *My joy may remain in you, and that your joy may be full.*"

Characteristics of the fruit of the Spirit—peace

Peace is that inner quietness and sense that God is in control. In Philippians 4:6-7, it states, "Be anxious for nothing, but in everything by prayer and supplication, with thanksgiving, let your requests be known to God; and *the peace of God*, which surpasses all understanding, will guard your hearts and minds through Christ Jesus." John writes in John 14:27, *"Peace I leave with you, My peace I give to you*; not as the world gives do I give to you. Let not your heart be troubled, neither let it be afraid."

Characteristics of the fruit of the Spirit—longsuffering

Longsuffering is literally translated "long temper." Fortunately, Jesus uses this special quality to insure our salvation. In 2 Peter 3:9, it says, "The Lord is not slack concerning His promise, as some count slackness, *but is longsuffering toward us*, not willing that any should perish but that all should come to repentance."

Characteristics of the fruit of the Spirit—patience

Patience is suffering without retaliation. Paul writes in Colossians 1:11, "Strengthened with all might, according to His glorious power, *for all patience* and longsuffering with joy." Also in Colossians 3:12, it says, "Therefore, as God's chosen people, holy and dearly loved, *clothe yourselves with compassion, kindness, humility, gentleness, and patience."* (NIV)

Characteristics of the fruit of the Spirit—kindness

Since God has shown His kindness to us through Jesus, we should be kind to each other. Ephesians 2:7 says, "That in ages to come He might show the exceeding riches of His grace *in His kindness toward us in Jesus Christ."* In 2 Corinthians 6:4 and 6 "But in all things we commend ourselves as ministers of God: ...by purity, by knowledge, by longsuffering, *by kindness*, by the Holy Spirit, by sincere love."

Characteristics of the fruit of the Spirit—goodness

Goodness is the practical application of love. In Ephesians 5:8-9, it says, "For you were once darkness, but now you are light in the Lord. Walk as children of light (for the *fruit of the Spirit is in all goodness*, righteousness, and truth)." If a man is truly good, he does good for others.

Characteristics of the fruit of the Spirit—faithfulness

Faithfulness is the quality of being faithful to our promises, duties, and obligations. This is evident in Luke 16: 10-12. Also in Matthew 25:21, it states, "His lord said to him, 'Well done good *and faithful servant*; you were faithful over a few things, I will make you ruler over many things. Enter into the joy of your lord.'"

Characteristics of the fruit of the Spirit—gentleness

Gentleness is slow to anger and slow to take offense. Jesus said in Matthew 11:29, "Take My yoke upon you and learn from Me, *for I am gentle* and lowly in heart, and you will find rest for your souls." Gentleness is not to be confused with cowardice or lack of leadership. Moses was the gentlest man in Israel, yet he exhibited great courage.

Characteristics of the fruit of the Spirit—self-control

Self-control is the ability to control the worldly part of our nature. In Proverbs 16:32, it says, *"He who is slow to anger is better than the mighty, and he who rules his spirit than he who takes a city."*

The question is: By which fruits are you known?

Chapter 7

He Will Teach You All Things.

The Holy Spirit is our Teacher.

The Holy Spirit's work is to bring to our memories the words of Christ and to teach us new truths. In John 14:26, it says, *"But the Helper, the Holy Spirit, whom the Father will send in My name, He will teach you all things, and bring to your remembrance all things that I said to you."*

The Holy Spirit brings to memory the words of Christ.

"And bring to your remembrance all things that I said to you." Jesus made this promise to the apostles, and it is the guarantee that their gospels are accurate. But it is also a promise to us. When we depend on the Holy Spirit, and look to Him, He provides the teachings of Christ when we need them. How often have we had a Scripture brought to mind while we were witnessing? That is the work of the Holy Spirit. The Greek word for remembrance, "hupomineskois," is better defined as "put into the mind of" implying an outside influence. In 2 Timothy 2:14, Paul writes to Timothy, *"Remind them of these things,* charging them before the Lord not to strive about words to no profit, to the ruin of the

hearers." In Luke 22:61, it says, "And the Lord turned and looked at Peter. *And Peter remembered the word of the Lord, how He said to him, 'Before the rooster crows, you will deny Me three times.'*" Jesus' words were put into the mind of Peter by the Holy Spirit.

The Holy Spirit will teach us all things.

In John 16:12-14, it states, "I still have many things to say to you, but you can not bear them now. However, *when He, the Spirit of truth, has come, He will guide you into all truth*; for He will not speak on His own authority, but whatever He hears He will speak; and He will tell you things to come. He will glorify Me, for He will take what is Mine and declare it to you." This promise was made to the apostles. But in 1 John 2:20, it states, "But you have an anointing from the Holy One, and you know all things." And in 1 John 2:27, it says, "But the anointing which you have received from Him abides in you, and you do not need that anyone teach you; *but as the same anointing teaches you concerning all things*, and is true, and is not a lie, and just as it has taught you, you will abide in Him." So we see that the Holy Spirit's teaching was not just for the apostles, but also for us today. In 1 John 2:27, we see that it is our privilege that we may be taught about God by God Himself through His Spirit. This, naturally, does not mean that we can not learn from others who teach by the Spirit. Intellectual teaching will not change you. Only teaching to our hearts by the Holy Spirit will bring a Christ-like character into us. Be open to what the Holy Spirit is saying to you. Have an ear to what the Spirit is saying!

The Holy Spirit guides us into truth.

In John 16:13, it states, "However, when He, the Spirit of truth, has come, He will guide you into all truth." The truth is found in the God's Word. The Holy Spirit reveals the hidden meaning of the Word; He makes the passages come alive with new meaning and clarity; the Bible is a spiritual book and requires a spiritual teacher. The Holy Spirit reveals the deep things of God, which are hidden from and considered foolishness to the natural man. In 1 Corinthians 2:9-13, it says, "But it is written: 'Eye has not seen, nor ear heard, nor have entered into the heart of man the things which God has prepared for those who love Him.' *But God has revealed them to us through His Spirit.* For the Spirit searches all things, yes, the deep things of God. For what man knows the things of a man except the spirit of man, which is in him? Even so no one knows the things of God except the Spirit of God. Now we have received, not the spirit of the world, but the Spirit who is from God, that we might know the things that have been freely given to us by God. These things we also speak, not in words which man's wisdom teaches but which the Holy Spirit teaches, comparing spiritual things with the spiritual." Isaiah 64:4, it states, "Eye has not seen, nor ear heard, nor have entered into the heart of man the things which God has prepared for those who love Him." *There is nothing on this earth that we can see, hear, or feel that compares with what God has prepared for those who love Him!*

The Holy Spirit gives us power to discern and compre-hend what He has taught us. In 1 Corinthians 2:14, Paul writes, "But the natural man does not receive the things of the Spirit of God, for they are foolishness to him; nor can he know them, because they are spiritually discerned." The Holy Spirit is not only the author of the Word, He is also the one who explains it. How wonderful that we have the author available to us! When we read the Word, we must do it in the spirit, not in the flesh. We must remove our inherent pride and ego and give ourselves entirely to the Spirit. It is the only way to write the Word on our hearts. In 1 Corinthians 3:18, it says, "Let no one deceive himself. If anyone among you seems to be wise in this age, let him become a fool that he may become wise." When we finally put away our own wisdom, and only then, do we receive the wisdom of God. We must also put away our own righteousness in order to receive God's righteousness. Paul writes in Romans 10:3, "For they being ignorant of God's righteousness, and seeking to establish their own righteousness, have not submitted to the righteousness of God."

The Holy Spirit enables us, the believers, to teach others the wisdom we have learned.

In 1 Corinthians 2:1-5, it states, "And I, brethren when I came to you, did not come with excellence of speech or of wisdom declaring to you the testimony of God. For I determined not to know anything among you except Jesus Christ and Him crucified. I was with you in weakness, in fear, and in much trembling. And my speech and my preaching were not with persuasive words of human wisdom, but in demonstration of the Spirit and of power, that your faith should not be in the wisdom of men but in the power of God." Also in 1 Thessalonians 1:5, it says, "For our gospel did not come to you in word only, but also in power, and in the Holy Spirit and in as much assurance, as you know what kind of men we were among you for your sake." The Holy Spirit revealed the truth to the apostles; He empowered them to write the truth in perfect remembrance; and He gave them, and us, the ability to communicate the truth effectively to others. **One great cause of our failure in God's service is our insistence to teach by human logic, persuasion, or eloquence what the Holy Spirit has taught us. We must take that step of faith, put ourselves entirely in the hands of the Holy Spirit and share our faith by His power.**

Chapter 8

The Baptism with the Holy Spirit

The greatest promise to mankind is in John 3:16 "For God so loved the world that He gave His only begotten Son, that whoever believes in Him should not perish but have everlasting life." But the greatest promise to believers is in Acts 1:8, where Jesus said, "But you shall receive power when the Holy Spirit has come upon you; and you shall be witnesses to Me in Jerusalem, and in all Judea and Samaria, and to the end of the earth." In Matthew 3:11 John the Baptist said, "I indeed baptize you with water unto repentance, but He who is coming after me is mightier than I, whose sandals I am not worthy to carry. He will baptize you with the Holy Spirit and fire." Also in Mark 1:8, "I indeed baptize you with water, but He will baptize you with the Holy Spirit." Jesus said in Acts 1:5, "For John truly baptized with water, but you shall be baptized with the Holy Spirit not many days from now." The experience is only referred to as the baptism *with* the Holy Spirit. It is not the baptism *of* the Holy Spirit.

The baptism experience

The baptism is a definite experience subsequent to salvation empowering us for His service. It is the Promise of the

Father. In Luke 24:49 Jesus said, "Behold, I send the Promise of My Father upon you; but tarry in the city of Jerusalem until you are endued with the power from on high." After His resurrection Jesus again instructed the apostles to wait for the power. Acts 1:4 says, "And being assembled together with them, He commanded them not to depart from Jerusalem, but to wait for the Promise of the Father, 'which,' He said, 'you have heard from Me.'" The baptism with the Holy Spirit is a promise from God.

A gift of the Holy Spirit.

In Acts 2:38 it says, "Then Peter said to them, 'Repent, and let every one of you be baptized in the name of Jesus Christ for the remission of sins; and you shall receive the *gift* of the Holy Spirit.'" The baptism is a free gift and cannot be earned. The baptism with the Holy Spirit is not a reward for service or other work. It is a gift of God's grace available for the asking.

It is the command of God.

If we are to be in God's service, and we all are in one form or another, then we are commanded by God to receive the baptism with the Holy Spirit. Acts 1:4 states, "And being assembled together with them, *He commanded them not to depart from Jerusalem, but to wait for the Promise of the Father,* 'which,' He said, 'you have heard from Me."

The primary purpose of the baptism with the Holy Spirit is to empower us for God's service.

In Acts 1:8, it says, "But you shall receive power when the Holy Spirit has come upon you; and you shall be witnesses to Me in Jerusalem, and in all Judea and Samaria, and to the end of the earth." Even Jesus was baptized with the Holy Spirit before He undertook His public ministry! Matthew 3:16-17 states, "Then Jesus, when He had been baptized, came up immediately from the water; and behold, the heavens were opened to Him, and He saw the Spirit of God descending like a dove and alighting upon Him." In Acts 10:38, Peter said, "How God anointed Jesus of Nazareth with the Holy Spirit and with power, who went about doing good and healing all who were oppressed by the devil, for God was with Him." Jesus promised the same power to his disciples, and to us, in John 14:12, "Most assuredly, I say to you, he who believes in Me, the works that I do he will do also; and greater works than these he will do, because I go to My Father."

Power and boldness were evident in the apostles after the baptism with the Holy Spirit.

After the crucifixion, the disciples were huddled together in fear in a closed room. John 20:19 says, "Then, the same day at evening, being the first day of the week, when the doors were shut where the disciples were assembled, for fear of the Jews." Yet after the baptism with the Holy Spirit, Peter and John went to the temple and preached (Acts, Chapter 3). Peter spoke boldly to the high priests in Acts 4:8, "Then Peter, filled with the Holy Spirit, said to them, Rulers of the people and elders of Israel." They were imprisoned for preaching Jesus. In Acts 5:17-18, it states, "The high priest rose up, and all those who were with him (which is the sect of the Sadducees), and they were filled with indignation, and laid their hands on the apostles and put them in the common prison." They were subsequently released from prison by angels and returned to the temple to resume preaching. Acts 5:19-20 states, "But at night an angel of the Lord opened the prison doors and brought them out, and said, 'Go, stand in the temple and speak to the people all the words of this life.'" They continued to preach and were once again arrested (Acts 5:25-39). In verse 40, they were beaten and commanded not to speak the name of Jesus. But verses 41 and 42 exemplify the power of the Holy Spirit, "So they departed from the presence of the council, rejoicing that they were counted worthy to suffer shame for His name. And daily in the temple, and in every house, *they did not cease teaching and preaching Jesus as the Christ.*"

Power for spiritual warfare.

God has commissioned us to do spiritual work, and this can only be accomplished by Spiritual power. Our efforts are being opposed by Satan, and we must be empowered for this spiritual battle. Ephesians 6:12 says, "For we do not wrestle against flesh and blood, but against principalities, against powers, against the rulers of the darkness of this age, against spiritual hosts of wickedness in the heavenly places." Paul continues in verse 17, "And take the helmet of salvation, and the *sword of the Spirit,* which is the word of God." Also in 2 Corinthians 10:3,4: "For though we walk in the flesh, we do not war according to the flesh. For the weapons of our warfare are not carnal but mighty in God for pulling down strongholds." Jesus said in Matthew 12:28, "But if *I cast out demons by the Spirit of God,* surely the kingdom of God has come upon you." Spiritual power for spiritual warfare.

The promise of its availability.

Jesus promised the apostles in Acts 1:5, "For John truly baptized with water, but you shall be baptized with the Holy Spirit not many days from now." He promised power in Acts 1:8, "But you shall receive power when the Holy Spirit has come upon you; and you shall be witnesses to Me in Jerusalem, and in all Judea and Samaria, and to the end of the earth."

The promise is fulfilled.

In Acts 2:4, Jesus' promise was fulfilled, "And they were all filled with the Holy Spirit and began to speak with other tongues, as the Spirit gave them utterance."

The baptism with the Holy Spirit was not just for the apostles.

In Acts 2:38-39, it says, "Then Peter said to them, 'Repent, and let every one of you be baptized in the name of Jesus Christ for the remission of sins; and you shall receive the gift of the Holy Spirit. For the promise is to you and to all your children, and to all who are afar off, as many as the Lord will call.'" In this passage of Scripture, Peter was addressing a large crowd, not the apostles, when he said, "For the promise is to you" The promise was definitely for people other than the apostles - "And to your children." The promise was definitely for the next generation - "And to all who are afar off." The promise was not only for those apostles, but for "all" in the future - "As many as the Lord will call." Also, in Acts 10, Peter entered Caesarea and went to the house of Cornelius where there were relatives and friends. Verse 24 says, "And the following day they entered Caesarea. Now Cornelius was waiting for them, and has called together his relatives and close friends." In verses 34-43, Peter addresses the gathering, and in verse 44, God delivered His promise to the Gentiles. Acts 10:44-45 says, "While Peter was still speaking these words, *the Holy Spirit fell upon all those who heard the word.* And those of the circumcision who believed were astonished, as many as came with Peter, *because the gift of the Holy Spirit has been poured out on the Gentiles also.*" Later in Jerusalem, Peter recounts the experience in Acts 11:15-16, "And as I began to speak, the Holy Spirit fell upon them, *as upon us in the beginning.* Then I remembered the word of the Lord, how He said, 'John indeed baptized with water, but you shall be baptized with the Holy Spirit.'" Clearly the baptism with the Holy Spirit is available to every believer. Also it is the same baptism that the apostles experienced, and is not diminished in any way. Acts 11:15 says, "The Holy Spirit fell upon them, as upon us in the beginning."

Another example of ordinary people receiving the baptism is in Acts 19:1-7. Here Paul travels to Ephesus and finds several believers, and he says in verse 2, "He said to them, 'Did you receive the Holy Spirit when you believed?' And they said to him, 'We have not so much as heard whether there is a Holy Spirit.'" Verse 6 continues, "And when Paul had laid hands on them, the Holy Spirit came upon them, and they spoke with tongues and prophesied."

Scripture is clear that the baptism with the Holy Spirit is available to every believer. Also, if God wanted the baptism only for the apostles, He would have made Scripture clear that it was only for them.

Receiving the baptism with the Holy Spirit.

When the multitude questioned Peter on how they may receive the power, he responded in Acts 2:37-38, "Now when they had heard this, they were cut to the heart, and said to Peter and the rest of the apostles, 'Men and brethren, what shall we do?'. Then Peter said to them 'Repent, and let every one of you be baptized in the name of Jesus Christ for the remission of sins; and you shall receive the gift of the Holy Spirit.'" In Acts 2:37, they asked Peter how they could receive the baptism, "Men and brethren, what shall we do?"

Repentance of sin and acceptance of Jesus Christ.

The first criteria is that we must be saved. In Acts 2:38, it says, "Then Peter said to them 'Repent, and let every one of you be baptized in the name of Jesus Christ for the remission of sins; and you shall receive the gift of the Holy Spirit.'"

We must ask for the baptism with the Holy Spirit.

Luke 11:13 says, "If you then being evil, know how to give good gifts to your children, how much more will your heavenly Father give the Holy Spirit to those who ask Him."

There must be hunger and thirst for more of God.

In Matthew 5:6, it says, "Blessed are those who hunger and thirst for righteousness, for they shall be filled." John 7:37-39 says, "On the last day, that great day of the feast, Jesus stood and cried out, saying 'If anyone thirsts, let him come to Me and drink. He who believes in Me, as the Scripture has said, out of his heart will flow rivers of living water.' But this He spoke concerning the Spirit, whom those believing in Him would receive; for the Holy Spirit was not yet given, because Jesus was not yet glorified."

We must believe by faith that we receive the baptism with the Holy Spirit.

James 1:6-8 says, "But let him ask in faith, with no doubting, for he who doubts is like a wave of the sea driven and tossed by the wind. For let not that man suppose that he will receive anything from the Lord; he is a doubled-minded man, unstable in all his ways."

Receiving the baptism with the Holy Spirit.

How the baptism is received is as individual as people themselves. There are no specific conditions outlined in Scripture, but basic truths are provided.

Receiving the baptism by faith In Galatians 3:14, Paul says clearly that it is by faith that we received the promise, "That the blessings of Abraham might come upon the Gentiles in Jesus Christ, that we might receive the promise of the Spirit through faith." Faith in the promises of God. Mark 11:24, "Therefore I say to you, whatever things you ask when you pray, believe that you will receive them, and you will have them." Do not be discouraged, but stand on the promises of God until the baptism is fully manifest.

We must fully yield ourselves to God.

The Word states that Jesus baptizes us with the Holy Spirit. In Luke 3:16, it says, "He will baptize you with the Holy Spirit and with fire." When we receive the baptism experience, we are yielding ourselves to Christ. The primary purpose of the Holy Spirit is to make known to us the fullness of Christ. But for that to happen, we must first be willing to make ourselves malleable, so that we may be changed. It is important to note that this does not mean that we should surrender our own personalities. The Holy Spirit does not replace our personalities, but rather works through our existing abilities and strengths. The Holy Spirit is Holy and will not dwell in an unclean house. Not that we are perfect, because we surely are not, but a willingness to continuously clean house is essential.

How the baptism is received.

There is no specific method for receiving the baptism, but there are several examples in Scripture: While sitting and expecting the Holy Spirit to come (Acts 2:1-4). While listening to the gospel being preached (Acts 10:44-46). [These men were not specifically expecting the baptism, but they obviously had open hearts to God's truth.] Praying and laying on of hands (Acts 8:14-17; 9:17; 19:6). Through our own faith and prayer (Luke 11:9-13; John 7:37-39).

Water baptism is not a condition for receiving the Holy Spirit.

It is clear in Acts 10:44-48 that the baptism with the Holy Spirit preceded a water baptism.

Speaking in tongues is the initial evidence of the baptism with the Holy Spirit.

God has given us this wonderful experience of the baptism. But because of our worldly nature and our inherent inclination to disbelieve, He has given us a clear sign. This sign is tongues. The baptism with the Holy Spirit is a spiritual experience manifested by a spiritual event. The Disciples spoke in tongues immediately after their baptisms. In Acts 2:4, says, *"And they were filled with the Holy Spirit and began to speak with other tongues, as the Spirit gave them utterance."*

Cornelius and his household were saved and received the baptism with the Holy Spirit with immediate evidence of tongues. Acts 10:43-46 says, "To Him all the prophets witness that, through His name, whoever believes in Him will receive remission of sins. While Peter was still speaking these words, the Holy Spirit fell upon all those who heard the word. And those of the circumcision who believed were astonished, as many as came with Peter, because the gift of the Holy Spirit has been poured out on the Gentiles also. For they heard them speak with tongues and magnify God. Then Peter answered." How did the Jews who came with Peter know that the Gentiles had received the baptism? They were at Pentecost and recognized the sign! Acts 10:45,46 states, "And those of the circumcision who believed were astonished, as many as came with Peter, because the gift of the Holy Spirit has been poured out on the Gentiles also. *For they heard them speak with tongues and magnify God."*

Another example is found in Acts 19:1-6, where Paul, while traveling in Ephesus, came upon believers who were saved but did not know of the empowering of the Holy Spirit. Acts 19: 2 states, "He said to them, 'Did you receive the Holy Spirit when you believed?' And they said to him, 'We have not so much as heard whether there is a Holy Spirit.'" Then Acts 19:6 says, "And when Paul had laid hands on them, the Holy Spirit came upon them, and they spoke with tongues and prophesied."

There were two other instances where tongues were not specifically mentioned, but were implied. Acts 8:17-19 does not specifically mention tongues, but Simon noticed evidence of the Holy Spirit that he was willing to pay for. Scripture reveals only one such type of recognizable evidence - tongues. Acts 8:17-19 says, "Then they laid hands on them, and they received the Holy Spirit. Now when Simon saw that through the laying on of the apostles' hands the Holy Spirit was given, he offered them money, saying, 'Give me this power also, that anyone on whom I lay hands may receive the Holy Spirit.'" Also, Acts 9:17 does not mention that Paul spoke in tongues when he received the baptism with the Holy Spirit, but it is clear that he did. 1 Corinthians 14:18 says, "I thank my God that I speak with tongues more than all of you."

Clearly, speaking in tongues is and, clearly, it is the result of a spiritual event ... the baptism with the Holy Spirit.

The nature and value of tongues.

Speaking in tongues is not only the initial evidence of the baptism, but also the means by which the blessings are manifested. Speaking in tongues is prayer and prayer brings forth God's blessings. The following are five scriptural references of the value of praying in tongues, which should lead us into regular and frequent communion with God.

The purpose of tongues is to speak to God.

In 1 Corinthians 14:2, Paul writes, "*For he who speaks in a tongue does not speak to men but to God*, for no one understands him; however, in the spirit he speaks mysteries."

We speak in a tongue we don't understand.

In 1 Corinthians 14:2, Paul writes, "For he who speaks in a tongue does not speak to men but to God, *for no one understands him*; however, in the spirit he speaks mysteries." Paul explains in 1 Corinthians 14:14, "For I pray in a tongue, my spirit prays, but my understanding is unfruitful." When we pray in tongues, the Holy Spirit gives our own spirits the words, and we utter them directly to God. It is truly a spiritual language because the body does not understand what is said. Also in Romans 8:26-27, it says, "Likewise the Spirit also helps in our weaknesses. For we do not know what we should pray for as we ought, but the Spirit Himself makes intercession for us with groanings which cannot be uttered. Now He who searches their hearts knows what the mind of the Spirit is, because He makes intercession for the saints according to the will of God."

Speaking in tongues builds us up spiritually.

In 1 Corinthians 4:4, it says, *"He who speaks in a tongue edifies himself,* but he who prophesies edifies the church." Jude 20 says, "But you, beloved, building yourselves up on your most holy faith, praying in the Holy Spirit, keep yourselves in the love of God, looking for the mercy of our Lord Jesus Christ unto eternal life."

We speak of the wonderful works of God.

In Acts 2:11, it states, "Cretans and Arabs - *we hear them speaking in our own tongues the wonderful works of God."*

Permanent evidence of the baptism with the Holy Spirit.

Jesus is revealed in us by the Holy Spirit. He was in our hearts at salvation, but not truly revealed. In John 16:13-15, it says, "However, when He, the Spirit of Truth, has come, He will guide you into all truth; for He will not speak on His own authority, but whatever He hears He will tell you things to come. *He will glorify Me, for He will take what is mine and declare it to you. All things that the Father has are min. Therefore I said that He will take Mine and declare it to you."*

A deep desire for people's salvation.

Immediately after Pentecost, the apostles did one thing - preached the gospel for the purpose of salvation. Three thousand people responded to Peter's preaching. Acts 2:42, says, *"Then those who gladly received his word were baptized; and that day about three thousand souls were added to them."* Again Peter, and John, while at the temple, preached the gospel of salvation. Acts 4:4 records, the result, "However, many of those who heard the word believed; and the number of the men came to about five thousand."

A power and boldness for witnessing.

This is evident in Acts 1:8, where Jesus says, *"But you shall receive power when the Holy Spirit has come upon you; and you shall be witnesses to Me in Jerusalem, and in Samaria, and to tend of the earth."*

A deep insight into God's Word.

The Holy Spirit is the only one who can give true insight into God's word. Again, in John 16:13-15, it says, "However, when He, the Spirit of Truth, has come, *He will guide you into all truth;* for He will not speak on His own authority, but whatever He hears He will tell you things to come. He will glorify Me, for He will take what is mine and declare it to you. All things that the Father has are Mine. Therefore I said that He will take of Mine and declare it to you."

Receiving the baptism by faith

In Galatians 3:14 Paul says clearly that it is by faith that we received the promise. "...that the blessings of Abraham might come upon the Gentiles in Jesus Christ, that we might receive the promise of the Spirit through faith." Also in John 7:39, it says, "But this He spoke concerning the Spirit, whom those believing in Him would receive...." Faith in the promises of God. Mark 11:24 sates, "Therefore I say to you, whatever things you ask when you pray, believe that you will receive them, and you will have them." Faith that the promise is for you. In Acts 2:39, it says, "For the promise is to you and to your children, and to all who are afar off, as many as the Lord our God will call." Faith that is persistent. Jesus in Luke 11:5-10 and 18:1-8 emphasized the importance of persistency of faith. The baptism is a life changing experience and there may be times that our motives may not be quite right. Do not be discouraged, but stand on the promises of God until the baptism is fully manifested.

How the baptism is received.

There is no specific method which to receive the baptism, but there are several examples in Scripture. While sitting and expecting the Holy Spirit to come as stated in Acts 2:1-4, "Now when the Day of Pentecost had fully come, *they were all with one accord in one place.* Suddenly there came a sound from heaven, as a rushing wind, and it filled the whole house where they were sitting. Then there appeared to them divided tongues, as of fire, and one sat upon each of them. *And they were all filled with he Holy Spirit and began to speak with other tongues, as the Spirit gave them utterance.*" People were baptize while listening to the gospel being preached. Acts 10:44,45 says, "*While Peter was still speaking these words, the Holy Spirit fell upon all those who heard the word.*" And those of the circumcision who believed were astonished, as many as came with Peter, because the gift of the Holy Spirit had been poured out on the Gentiles also." The baptism was also received by praying and laying on of hands as stated in Acts 8:14-17, "Now when the apostles who were at Jerusalem heard that Samaria had received the word of God, they sent Peter and John to them, who, when they had come down, prayed for them that they might receive the Holy Spirit. For as yet He had fallen upon none of them. They had only been baptized in the name of Lord Jesus. *Then they laid hands on them, and they received the Holy Spirit.*" Examples of laying on of hands can also be found in Acts 9:17 and 19:6. Jesus stated it can also be received by our own faith and prayer. In Luke 11:9-13, it says, "If a son asks for bread from any father among you, will he give him a stone? Or if he asks for a fish, will he give him a serpent instead of a fish? Or if he asks for an egg, will he offer him a scorpion? If you then, being evil, know how to give good gifts to your children, *how much more will your heavenly Father give the Holy Spirit to those who ask Him!*"

Ministering the baptism with the Holy Spirit.

There is no specific method of ministering the baptism with speaking in tongues, but the following may be helpful.

Share the gospel.

Explain what the Word says about the baptism and the coming forth in tongues. It is important they understand that speaking in tongues is scriptural.

Explain to them what to expect from the baptism.

Explain what God's word says concerning the baptism. They should be encouraged to receive the baptism now.

Lead them in prayer.

Pray with the believer because the Word states that we must ask for the promise.

Focus the attention on Jesus.

Jesus is the one who baptizes with the Holy Spirit. We should focus the believer's attention on Jesus, praising and worshiping Him.

Encourage the believer to come forth in tongues.

Encourage the believer to start using their new prayer language. Encourage them to start by making sounds and pray with them in tongues.

What if the believer does not speak in tongues.

Speaking in any language requires actually opening the mouth and uttering the words. Encourage speaking in audible sounds and start with simple words. A language is made up of words, but we must first establish the words. Ensure that the believer has the faith to receive the gift of tongues. Reassure them of what God's Word says about tongues. Address their embarrassment. Speaking strange sounds in front people can be embarrassing. Be understanding, comforting, and try to get them to relax. It is important to be encouraging. Assure the believer that it is God's will that they speak in tongues and even small syllables is a start to their prayer language. If they do not speak in tongues try to prevent discouragement. Some people do not receive tongues immediately and encourage them continue to try to develop the gift on their own. God will certainly bless them with the tool that strengthens and empowers. Encourage them to give thanks to God for this wonderful gift. Encourage the believer to pray and sing in tongues daily (1 Corinthians 14:15).

Fillings with the Holy Spirit.

The baptism with the Holy Spirit leads to a Spirit filled life, but to continually operate in the power of the Holy Spirit, we need to be continuously filled. *There is one baptism but many fillings.*

Fillings for defending the faith.

Peter spoke to the Sanhedrin with power in Acts 4:8 "Then Peter, filled with the Holy Spirit, said to them, 'Rulers of the people and elders of Israel....'" Jesus predicted such power in Luke 12:11-12 "Now when they bring you to the synagogues and magistrates and authorities, do not worry about what you should say. For the Holy Spirit will teach you in that very hour what you ought to say."

Fillings for rebuking Satan.

We can expect special fillings for the battle against the Devil. Paul confronted a sorcerer in Acts 13:9,10 "Then Saul, who was also called Paul, *filled with the Holy Spirit* looked intently at him and said, 'O full of all deceit and all fraud, you son of the devil, you enemy of all righteousness, will you not cease perverting the straight ways of the Lord?"

Fillings for new boldness and power.

The Sanhedrin had just rebuked and threatened the disciples, but with a new filling, they were able to preach the Word with boldness and power. Acts 4:31 "And when they had prayed, the place where they were assembled together was shaken; *and they were all filled with the Holly Spirit, and they spoke the word of God with boldness.*"

Fillings to endure persecutions for the sake of the gospel.

The disciples were having great success in delivering the message of salvation in Antioch and Pisidia, but were persecuted for it. In Acts 13:50-52, it says, "But the Jews stirred up the devout and prominent women and the chief men of the city, raised up persecution against Paul and Barnabas, and expelled them from their region. But they shook off the dust from their feet against them, and came to Iconium. *And the disciples were filled with joy and with the Holy Spirit.*"

Chapter 9

Gifts of the Holy Spirit

The purpose of the gifts.

The purpose of the gifts is to equip and to edify us.

To equip us.

In Ephesians 4:12, it says *"...for the equipping of the saints for the work of the ministry,* for the edifying of the body of Christ." The Holy Spirit gives us gifts so that we may be equipped for His service.

To edify us.

"...for the edifying of the body of Christ." The Greek *oikodome* means the "act of building a structure". The gifts are to be used to build the house of the Lord.

Using the gifts.

First, Paul states that we should desire the gifts. In 1 Corinthians 12:31, it states, "But earnestly desire the best gifts." After we desire them, we should pray for the gifts. However, it is God who determines who receives which gift, and in what portion. Hebrews 2:4 says, "God also bearing witness both with signs and wonders, with various miracles, *and gifts of the Holy Spirit, according to His own will?"* Once we received the gift, we must use it! In Matthew 25:29, Jesus explains the parable of the talents, "For to everyone who has, more will be given, and he will have abundance; but from him who does not have, even what he has will be taken away." Jesus gives us these gifts for the benefit of the body, and if we do not use them, they might be taken away. The gifts would be exercised with humility because it is not our own power that these abilities come forth, but by God's grace for the furtherance of His Kingdom. Above all, seek the source Himself. Jesus says in Matthew 6:33, "But seek first the kingdom of God and His righteousness, and all these things shall be added to you.".

The gifts of 1 Corinthians 12.

In 1 Corinthians 12:4-13, it states, "Now there are diversities of gifts, but the same Spirit. There are differences of ministries, but the same Lord. And there are diversities of activities, but it is the same God who works in all. But the manifestation of the Spirit is given to each one for the profit of all: for to one is given the word of wisdom through the Spirit, to another the word of knowledge through the same Spirit, to another faith by the same Spirit, to another gifts of healings by the same Spirit, to another the working of miracles, to another prophecy, to another discerning of spirits, to another different kinds of tongues, to another the interpretation of tongues. But one and the same Spirit works all these things, distributing to each one individually as He wills. For as the body is one and has many members, but all the members of that one body, being many, are one body, so also is Christ. For by one Spirit we were all baptized into one body-whether Jews or Greeks, whether slaves or free - and have all been made to drink into one Spirit."

Word of wisdom.

The word of wisdom is not the gift of wisdom, such as Solomon possessed. It is also not necessarily a vocal gift. The Greek word logos means concept, or idea, or subject matter. Stephen operated with a word of wisdom in Acts 6:10 "And they were not able to resist the wisdom and the Spirit by which he spoke." The word of wisdom reveals God's mind or will, or how to carry out His will. Wisdom brings forth understanding.

Word of knowledge.

The word of knowledge reveals information about a person, place or thing. As opposed to the word of wisdom, which reveals insight. Peter operated under a word of knowledge in Acts 5:1-6 where he knew that Ananias and his wife withheld part of the money.

Special faith.

In Hebrews 11:1, it says "Now faith is the substance of things hoped for, the evidence of things not seen." This special faith is different than the normal Christian faith in God. It is the gift of faith that believes that God can and will do, what we in our limited humanity, cannot do. Special faith accompanies healings and miracles. In Acts chapter 3, Peter had the special faith that healed the lame man. Jesus talked about special faith in Mark 11:22-24 "So Jesus answered and said to them, "Have faith in God. For assuredly, I say to you, whoever says to this mountain, 'Be removed and be cast into the sea,' and does not doubt in his heart, but believes that those things he says will come to pass, he will have whatever he says. Therefore I say to you, whatever things you ask when you pray, believe that you receive them, and you will have them." In verse 22 "Have faith in God." literally translates "Have the faith of God."

Gifts of healings.

In the original Greek both words, gifts and healings are plural. This implies that each healing is a separate gift of the Holy Spirit. A gift of healing (singular) would imply that the believer would be able to heal all the time. This is not scriptural. Although healing was very common in the ministry of Jesus and the apostles, not every person was healed. In Mat 13:58 Jesus did not perform "mighty works" in His own town because of unbelief. Special faith is essential for healings. In Luke 7:1-10 Jesus heals the servant of a centurion, just by declaring him healed. It was the special faith of the centurion that allowed the healing to take place. Jesus said in Luke 7:9 "When Jesus heard these things, He marveled at him, and turned around and said to him, 'I say to you, I have not found such great faith, not even in Israel." In the Great Commission of Mark 16:15-18, Jesus states in verse 17 "And these signs will follow those who believe:...", not just the apostles, but "...those who believe:..". Further in verse 18 He says "...they will lay hands on the sick and they will recover.". The laying on of hands is an outward sign of inward belief that God will heal them.

Working of miracles.

The Greek, *energemata dunameon*, is literally translated "operations of supernatural power." As with the gifts of healings, both words are plural. Also, as with the gifts of healings, each miracle is caused by faith. In Hebrews 2:4 "God also bearing witness both with signs and wonders, with various miracles, and gifts of the Holy Spirit, according to His own will?" God, through the Holy Spirit, bears witness to Jesus Christ by these "signs and wonders." The New Testament has many examples of the signs, wonders, and miracles: Deliverance from imprisonment (Acts 5:18-20, 12:5-10, 16:23-30); Sudden blindness of Elymas the sorcerer (Acts 13:8-12); Philip being instantly moved from one place to another (Acts 9:36-42); The raising of the dead of Dorcas (Acts 9:36-42) and Eutychus (Acts 20:9-12); Paul's surviving the poisonous snake bite (Acts 28:3-5).

Gift of prophecy.

The gift of prophecy is different than the office of prophet. Not all can occupy the office of prophet as Paul states in Eph 4:11 "And He Himself gave some to be apostles, some prophets, some evangelists, and some pastors and teachers...." The prophecy gift can predict future events as in Acts 21:11: "When he had come to us, he took Paul's belt, bound his own hands and feet, and said, 'Thus says the Holy Spirit, So shall the Jews at Jerusalem bind the man who owns this belt, and deliver him into the hands of the Gentiles." The gift also edifies, exhorts, and comforts the body of Christ in 1 Cor. 14:3: "But he who prophesies speaks edification and exhortation and comfort to men." Also in Acts 15:32: "Now Judas and Silas, themselves being prophets also, exhorted the brethren with many words and strengthened them."

Discerning of spirits

The gift of discerning of spirits is the ability to tell the difference between work of the Holy Spirit and the work of evil spirits. Paul exercised this gift in Acts 16:16-18: "Now it happened, as we went to prayer, that a certain slave girl possessed with a spirit of divination met us, who brought her masters much profit by fortunetelling. This girl followed Paul and us, and cried out, saying, 'These men are servants of the Most High God, who proclaim to us the way of salvation.' And this she did for many days. But Paul, greatly annoyed, turned and said to the spirit, 'I command you in the name of Jesus Christ to come out of her.' And he came out that very hour." The gift of discerning spirits is not the judging of people, but rather judging the spirit behind the manifestation.

Kinds of tongues.

This gift is different than the prayer language resulting from the baptism with the Holy Spirit. This gift of a new language is to used in public, but must be accompanied by interpretation 1Cor 14:5 "I wish you all spoke with tongues, but even more that you prophesied; for he who prophesies is greater than he who speaks with tongues, unless indeed he interprets, that the church may receive edification." This tongue is used for the edification of the body of Christ. 1Cor 14:22 "Therefore tongues are for a sign, not to those who believe but to unbelievers; but prophesying is not for unbelievers but for those who believe." This gift is used a "sign and wonder" to the unbeliever for the purpose of salvation.

Interpretation of tongues.

First Corinthians 14:5 says, "I wish you all spoke with tongues, but even more that you prophesied; for he who prophesies is greater than he who speaks with tongues, unless indeed he interprets, that the church may receive edification." The public utterance of a tongue must be accompanied by interpretation. 1Cor 14:16-17 "Otherwise, if you bless with the spirit, how will he who occupies the place of the uninformed say 'Amen' at your giving of thanks, since he does not understand what you say. For you indeed give thanks well, but the other is not edified." All gifts are to be used for God's glory, not ours.

Gifts of Ephesians 4

It says in Ephesians 4:11-12: "And He Himself gave some to be apostles, some prophets, some evangelists, and some pastors and teachers, for the equipping of the saints for the work of the ministry, for the edifying of the body of Christ." When God calls a believer into one of these offices, He first equips him with the appropriate spiritual gift.

The apostle.

The Greek word is *apostolos* meaning "one sent forth", and the office was not just for the original twelve. In Romans 1:1, it says, "Paul, a servant of Jesus Christ, *called to be an apostle*, separated to the gospel of God." The apostle preaches, teaches, testifies, and exhorts. Acts 2:40-42 states, *"and with many other words he testified and exhorted them* saying, 'Be saved from this perverse generation.' Then those who gladly received his word were baptized; and that day about thee thousand souls were added to them. And they continued steadfastly in the apostles' doctrine and fellowship, in the breaking of bread, and in prayers." The apostle assists in staring new churches, strengthening believers, and appointing leaders. In Acts 14:21-23, it states, "And when they had preached the gospel to that city and made many disciples, they returned to Lystra, Iconium, and Antioch, strengthening the souls of the disciples, exhorting them to continue in the faith, and saying, 'We must through many tribulations enter the kingdom of God.' So when they had appointed elders in every church, and prayed with fasting, they commended them to the Lord in whom they had believed."

The prophet.

The word prophet means "one who speaks openly a divine message." The message is given to the prophet by the Holy Spirit. It says in Ephesians 3:1-5, it says, "For this reason I, Paul, the prisoner of Jesus Christ for you Gentiles— if indeed you have heard of the dispensation of the grace of God which was given to me for you, how that by revelation He made known to me the mystery (as I wrote before in a few word, by which, when you read, you may understand my knowledge in the mystery of Christ), which other ages was not made known to the sons of men, *as it has now been revealed by the Spirit to His holy apostles and prophets*: ..." An example is given in Acts 11:27-28, where it says, "And in these days prophets came from Jerusalem to Antioch. Then one of them, named Agabus, stood up and showed by the Spirit that there was going to be a great famine throughout the world, which also happened in the days of Caesar." Not all prophets are of God and we must be discerning. In 1 John 4:1, it says, "Beloved, do not believe every spirit, but test the spirits, whether they are of God; because many false prophets have gone into the world."

The evangelist.

The word evangelist comes from the Greek *euangelistes*, which means "one who proclaims good news." Our word gospel translates from another form of the same Greek word. The ministry of Philip, who was specifically called an evangelist in Acts 21:8, is clearly described in Acts chapter 8. The evangelist preaches the gospel. In Acts 8:5, it states, "The Philip went down to the city of Samaria and preached Christ to them." Also where Philip encounters the eunuch in verse 35: "Then Philip opened his mouth, and beginning at this Scripture, preached Jesus to him." The work of the evangelist results in many people coming to Christ. Acts 8:6: "And multitudes with one accord heeded the things spoken by Philip, hearing and seeing the miracles which he did." And in Acts 8:12, it says, "But when they believed Philip as he preaches the things concerning the kingdom of God and the name of Jesus Christ, both men and women were baptized." The ministry of an evangelist includes casting out demons and healing of the sick. In Acts 8:6-7, it states, "And multitudes with one accord heeded the things spoken by Philip, hearing and seeing the miracles which he did. For unclean spirits, crying with a loud voice, came out of many who were possessed; and many who were paralyzed and lame were healed." In Acts 8:40, it states, "But Philip was found at Azotus. And passing through, he preached in all the cities till he came to Caesarea."

The pastor.

The Greek word *poimen* is defined as shepherd. A shepherd is one who takes care of his flock by feeding and caring for them. The pastor feeds the flock. In John 21:15-17 Jesus gives these commands: verse 15 "...'Feed My lambs." Verse 16: "...'Tend My sheep." Verse 17 "...'Feed My sheep." The feeding is teaching the Word. In 1 Peter 2:2, it says, "...as newborn babes, desire the pure milk of the word, that you may grow thereby...." The pastor leads his flock. In Acts 20:28, it states, "Therefore take heed to yourselves and to all the flock, among which the Holy Spirit has made you overseer, to shepherd the church of God which He purchased with His own Blood." The pastor is also to lead by example. In 1 Timothy 4:12, it states, "Let no one despise your youth, but be an example to the believers in word, conduct, in love, in spirit, in faith, in purity." The pastor guards his flock. In Acts 20:28-30, it says, "Therefore take heed to yourselves and to all the flock, among which the Holy Spirit has made you overseer, to shepherd the church of God which He purchased with His own blood. For I know this, that after my departure savage wolves will come in among you, not sparing the flock. Also from among yourselves men will rise up, speaking perverse things, to draw away the disciples after themselves." The pastor exhorts his flock. Hebrews 13:17 states, "Obey those who rule over you, and be submissive, for they watch out for your souls, as those who must give account."

The teacher.

In Ephesians 4:11, Paul refers to "pastors and teachers" as one position. This does not mean that the words are interchangeable. There can be a teacher who is not a pastor, but there cannot be a pastor who is not a teacher. The Greek word *didaskalos* means an instructor. An evangelist comes into a city and brings the lost to Christ, but it is up to the local pastor-teacher to feed the newborn sheep. Teaching is part of the Great Commission. In Matthew 28:19-20, it says, "Go, therefore and make disciples of all nations, baptizing them in the name of the Father and of the Son and of the Holy Spirit, teaching them to observe all things that I have commanded you; and lo, I am with you always, even to the end of the age." The teacher is to teach sound doctrine. Titus 1:9 says,"...holding fast the faithful word as he has been taught, that he may be able, by sound doctrine, both to exhort and convict those who contradict." The teacher is to true to the Word. In 2 Timothy 2:15, Paul writes, "Be diligent to present yourself approved to God, a worker who does not need to be ashamed, rightly dividing the word of truth."

The gifts of 1 Corinthians 12:28-31.

In 1 Corinthians 12:28-31, it says, "And God has appointed these in the church: first apostles, second prophets, third teachers, after that miracles, then gifts of healings, helps, administrations, varieties of tongues. Are all apostles? Are all prophets? Are all teachers? Are all workers of miracles? Do all have gifts of healings? Do all speak in tongues? Do all interpret? But earnestly desire the best gifts. And yet I show you a more excellent way." Paul, in this passage, talks of the three ministry gifts of Ephesians 4, and also reiterates six of the gifts mentioned earlier in the chapter 12. However, he also talks of two new gifts: the gift of helps and the gift of administration.

The gift of helps.

In Acts 9:36, it states, "At Joppa there was a certain disciple named Tabitha, which is translated Dorcas. This woman was full of good works and charitable deeds which she did." Also in Acts 20:35, it states, "I have shown you in every way, by laboring like this, that you must support the weak. And remember the words of the Lord Jesus, that He said, 'It is more blessed to give than to receive." The gift of helps is for support and assistance for those people who need help of any kind, but especially the week or those in special need.

The gift of administration

The gift of administration is the ability to guide the church. The Greek *kubernesis* is literally translated "government", but in another form is translated master or shipmaster. No man can guide a church in his humanity. Only God, through the Holy Spirit, can guide and direct the course a church should take.

Author Bio

R ichard A. Ingui is Senior Pastor of River of Hope Fellowship in Malta, New York. He and his wife, Nancy, pastor a church that is experiencing wonderful growth. Pastor Rich has been studying the Holy Spirit for much of his Christian life.

He and his wife host a weekly radio show in the Albany, New York, area. The show has been on the air since 1998 and is a live call-in prayer show.

Printed in the United States
52191LVS00004B/385-579

9 781597 819961